The Traditional TURNOUT

Fitting the Horse, Carriage, Harness, Appointments,
Whip, Passengers, and Groom

Gloria Austin's Collection of Books

Gloria Austin is an award winning preservationist, carriage collector, and holds many championship titles.

www.GloriaAustin.com

ENJOY OUR OTHER BOOKS

- The Brewster Story
- Carriage Lamps
- Gloria Austin's Carriage Collection
- A Glossary of Harness Parts
- Equine Elegance
- The Fire Horse
- Horse Basics 101
- Westward Ho!
- The Unsung Heros of World War One
- The Horse, History, and Human Culture
- Horse Symbolism
- Horses of the Americas
- A Drive Through Time
- The Medieval Horse
- Speak Your Horse's Language
- Tea: Steeped in Tradition
- Woman and Horses
- The Golden Carriage and the House of Hapsburg
- Horses and Newport
- A Cookbook for Horse Lovers
- Dance! To Improve Riding and Driving

Brought To You By The Equine Heritage Institute

The Traditional Turnout
Fitting the Horse, Carriage, Harness, Appointments, Whip, Passengers, and Groom
By: Gloria Austin President of Equine Heritage Institute, Inc. (EHI)

First Publish Date 2020
Copyright © 2020 by Equine Heritage Institute, Inc.

All rights reserved. No part of this publication may be reproduced, distributed, or transmitted in any form or by any means, including photocopying, recording, or other electronic or mechanical methods, without the prior written permission of the publisher, except in the case of brief quotations embodied in critical reviews, and certain other noncommercial uses permitted by copyright law. For permission requests, write to the publisher, addressed "Attention: Permissions Coordinator,"
at the address below.

Gloria Austin Carriage Collection, LLC; Equine Heritage Institute, Inc.
3024 Marion County Road Weirsdale, FL 32195 Office: (352) 753-2826 Fax: (352) 753-6186

Ordering Information:
Quantity sales: Special discounts are available on quantity purchases by corporations, associations, and others. For details, contact the publisher at the address above.
Printed in the United States of America First Edition
ISBN: 978-1-951895-21-1

TABLE OF CONTENTS

- 8   Introduction
- 9   What is "Turnout"?
- 10 Puttin' on the Ritz
- 12 Classification of Turnouts
    - 12 The Purpose
    - 15 The Driver
    - 18 The Horses/Ponies
- 22 Parts of the Turnout
    - 22 Carriages
    - 37 Appointments
    - 42 The People
        - 42 The Whip (Driver)
        - 48 The Coachman and Grooms
        - 50 The Guard
        - 50 The Horn Sounder
        - 51 The Passengers
        - 52 The Dog
    - 54 Harness
    - 57 The Horses
- 58 Putting It All Together
- 88 Rules for Turnouts
- 98 Gloria's Turnouts
- 106 Sources

SPECIAL THANKS TO OUR TEAM

Mary Chris Foxworthy, Research Writer

Mary Chris' grandfather owned one of the last creameries in the United States that still used horse-drawn milk wagons. This sparked her life-long love affair with horses and passion for keeping horse history alive. After graduating from college with a degree in Food Science and Communications, Mary Chris bought her very first horse with her first paycheck. Since then, she has served on the board of various equine associations and held a judge's card in Carriage Driving. She is known for her work in the Gloria Austin Collection, and has published and presented numerous equine educational programs. She has written for several equine publications and won an award from American Horse Publications for one of her articles. Mary Chris is an active exhibitor in Carriage Driving and Dressage. Along with her husband, she enjoys spending time with their horses (two Morgans and a PRE), a bouncing Bearded Collie and two adult children and one grandchild.

BROUGHT TO YOU BY

The books created by Equine Heritage Institute are designed to preserve the history and majesty of the horse. Our goal is to find, understand, and pass on the valuable data about equine use and its influence on humanity. The Equine Heritage Institute is a not for profit 501(c)(3) and 100% of all proceeds from the sale of books, services, and products support Equine Heritage Institute's mission.

To make a donation to EHI, please visit EHI-store.square.site/s/shop

A COPY OF THE OFFICIAL REGISTRATION AND FINANCIAL INFORMATION MAY BE OBTAINED FROM THE DIVISION OF CONSUMER SERVICES BY CALLING TOLL-FREE WITHIN THE STATE REGISTRATION DOES NOT IMPLY ENDORSEMENT, APPROVAL, OR RECOMMENDATION BY THE STATE.   s. 496.411, F.S.

1-800-HELP-FLA (435-7352)   www.FloridaConsumerHelp.com

The Horse

"We have had 6,000 years of history with the domesticated horse and only 100 years with the automobile."
Gloria Austin

INTRODUCTION

The many vehicles on today's highways all serve specific purposes. Pick-up trucks were originally used as an agricultural beast of burden. Today, trucks are both a tool for labor as well as a source of amusement for those who enjoy "off-roading". Sports cars are performance vehicles that provide driving satisfaction and pleasure. Some people require a combination of pulling capacity and passenger seating and the SUV fits the bill for that. Mini-vans are for those who need passenger space. Sedans offer comfort and often times, luxury. There are vehicles for every need!

In the past, horse drawn carriages were a major form of conveyance. Just as vehicles on the road today serve specific purposes, so did the many carriages that were used. Each carriage was turned out to suit the specific use of that carriage. The horse, harness, appointments and even clothing of the driver and passengers all served a purpose. The Runabout was the pick-up truck of the past and the Gig was the sports car. Today, many of these carriages of the past are still in use and can be seen at horse shows and at Concours d'Elegance events. They are meticulously turned out just as they were in the past but with contemporary attire. Understanding the history and purpose of carriages is part of knowing how to correctly turn out the carriage. So park your pick-up, min-van or sports car and find a cozy chair to enjoy The Pleasure Driving Turnout.

1958 Chevrolet Corvette

1870 Flandrau Gig

WHAT IS TURNOUT ?

Turnout is defined as the combination of horse(s), carriage, harness, appointments, driver (whip), passenger(s) and groom(s). There are many things to consider when putting a turnout together:

The fit
- Does the horse fit the carriage?
- Does the harness fit the horse?
- Appropriateness
- Is the horse the correct type for the carriage?
- Is the harness the correct type of harness for the carriage?
- Are the whip, passengers and grooms properly attired?
- Are the appointments correct for the carriage?
- Overall Impression
- Do the horses move well with confidence and ease?
- Is the whip relaxed and confident too?
- Are the grooms doing their jobs efficiently?

"PUTTIN' ON THE RITZ"

At this point you might be wondering, "where and when would any of this matter?"

There are many opportunities for owners of horses and traditional carriages to "put on the Ritz" and enjoy their passion for horses and history!

The American Driving Society (ADS) writes the rules for carriage driving. The rules are based on historical research, practicality and safety. Pleasure Driving is meant to replicate driving as it was when horses were used for pleasure driving. The ADS says, "Pleasure Driving is a show ring competition. Horses and/or ponies are hitched to antique vehicles or replicas." In Europe it is called "Private Driving".

Pleasure Driving Carriage Shows will have a Turnout Class. A type of carriage called a pleasure carriage is used as opposed to a farm or commercial wagon or a utility (marathon) carriage.

The ADS rules for a Turnout Class state that it is:
"A Pleasure Driving class in which entries are judged primarily on the performance and quality of each turnout. The turnout is to be shown both ways of the arena at a walk, slow trot, working trot, and strong trot.

The turnout must also stand quietly and rein back. The class is judged
- 70% on the condition, fit and appropriateness of harness and vehicle, spares and appointments, neatness and appropriateness of attire and overall impression.
- 30% on performance, manners and way of going."

Traditional carriages are also enjoyed on Recreational Drives. There are many driving clubs that organize such events. As with Pleasure Driving at shows, Recreational Driving requires a sturdy carriage and a well-fitted, comfortable harness. Any breed of horse, pony, donkey or mule that is bred to walk, trot, amble or canter may participate. The American Driving Society offers awards for cumulative hours of driving by its members. Driving clubs from around the world may have individual standards and safety rules for its these events. The National Drive is held at various locations across the US every year; it is an event that welcomes all.

Picnic drives are often enjoyed with traditional carriages as well and some shows even over classes where the turnout of the picnic is judged too. Modern football tailgating came from the age-old custom of lowering the tailgate of the boot of a large coach.

Combined Driving Events (CDE) use a carriage that is modern and utilitarian. Combined Driving is a versatility test with each of the three phases of the competition having its own objective. The three phases are:

- Dressage
- Marathon
- Cones

Turnout is still important in each phase of a CDE while the Marathon portion allows the competitors to have a little fun with more causal attire.

CLASSIFICATION OF TURNOUTS
THE PURPOSE

Turnouts may be classified by the purpose of the turnout. These purposes are:
- State (Gala)
- Town (Formal)
- Country (Sporting)
- Family
- Commercial

Just as there are many models of cars today, there were many types of carriages. The lists here are just a small representation of the many types of carriages within each classification.

State/Gala

The most important part of the collection of carriages used by royal families are state coaches, ceremonial and gala carriages. They are often richly decorated with ornate carving and painting. The weight of these carriages is usually more than 8000 pounds so they are pulled by six to eight horses and can usually only proceed at a walking pace; which after-all is favorable since it's about being seen! When one looks at the variety of royal carriages throughout history, a number of adjectives spring to mind: magnificent, spectacular, sumptuous, resplendent. These are palaces on wheels—symbols of majesty and power—and perfect for making a grand entrance. (*cited from: https://fiveminutehistory.com/royal-carriages-traveling-in-splendor/*)

Entrance of the Emperor Franz I. Stephan and his son Joseph (II.) into Frankfurt on March 29, 1764 by Johann Dallinger von Dalling, 1767

Town/Formal

An almost bewildering variety of horse-drawn carriages existed in the past. One's choice of carriage was only in part based on practicality and performance; it was also a status statement and subject to changing fashions and the Town/Formal vehicles were a prime example of a status statement. A few of the carriages that fit into this category include:

- Phaeton
- Gig
- Landau
- Brougham
- Victoria

Central Park 1890s

Country

Carriages that were used in the country were often used for sporting purposes. For instance in the 1890s, the term "shooting-brake" was coined to describe a long, boxy, horse-drawn carriage that would be used to ferry about shooting parties. In other parts of the world, that would be called hunting 'brake' derived from the Dutch word, "brik", meaning 'cart' or 'carriage'. It needed to be large enough to carry not only the shooting party, but also all their guns, ammunition and the game they had killed. *(cited from: https://medium.com/@zacknorman97/shot-chaser-maserati-alfieri-shooting-brake-concept-d5992acf758a)* Country carriages include:

- Shooting Breack
- Meadowbrook Cart
- Dog Cart
- Cocking Cart
- Wagonette

Family

Family vehicles of today include station wagons, vans and SUVs. They serve a purpose of transporting people and groceries or merchandise. Family carriages of the past performed the same function. The Concord wagon for instance was very utilitarian. The curved shape of the body of the carriage allowed for packages to bounce to the middle of the carriage rather than bounce out. Some family type carriages include:

- Governess cart
- Surrey
- Runabout
- Concord Wagon

1872 Concord Wagon - notice the curved body

Commercial

Buses transport people around cities, delivery trucks bring packages to our homes and "big rigs", on the highways, carry large amounts of cargo. Before motorized vehicles, horses and carriages were used for these purposes. Some vehicles were used to transport people and goods cross country and some were used within the city for home delivery or to move goods from train depots to businesses. Commercial carriages include:

- Mountain Wagon
- Omnibus
- Barge
- Stagecoach
- Steam Pumper (and many other fire apparatus)
- Delivery Wagons (Ice, Milk, Oil, etc.)

Early 1900s Milk Wagon - it was often said that the horse could do the route without the driver!

CLASSIFICATION OF TURNOUTS
THE DRIVER

Today Mom drives a mini van, Grandpa drives a sedan, a tillerman drives the back of a hook and ladder truck and someone with a CDL (commercial driver's license) is allowed to operate large, heavy, or placarded hazardous material vehicles in commerce. Other than the big rigs, we do not normally classify vehicles today by the person who is driving the vehicle. However, carriage Turnouts can be classified by the person who drives the carriage. These classifications are:

- Owner (Gentleman or Lady or Youth)
- Servant (Coachman or Governess)
- Postilion

Owner

The driver sits on the right (which would be the same as the passenger side in an American car). If there is a groom they may be seated next to the driver or behind the driver if there is a rear position.

Servant Driven

On a *Full State Carriage* the coachman sits on the hammer cloth on the front. The passengers sit inside. Since America did not have nobility, these types of carriages were not found in America.

Owned and restored by Gloria Austin, this restored Armbruster Dress Chariot is the only full state carriage in the world in private ownership.

A Victoria is also a type of carriage driven by a coachman. The passengers sit behind the coachman. In this photo Queen Victoria is the passenger and John Brown is siting in front with the coachman. Some Victorias are also owner driven

A Governess Cart is a type of vehicle that a governess would use to transport the children in her care.

On a Dress Landau the driver's seat is elevated and the passengers sit facing each other.

The *Hansom Cab* is a two-wheeled vehicle with a body hung very close to the ground, affording easy access to passengers through twin doors in the front of the cab. The driver's seat is high up and behind the body of the vehicle. The driver could open and shut the passenger doors from where he sat. The Hansom Cab was used primarily as a public vehicle and became the cab of choice in most major cities of England and America. There were, however, some private Hansoms. *(cited from: https://web.archive.org/web/20071027142250/http://www.caaonline.com/caa_content.asp?PageType=Dept&Key=15&MCat=7)*

The Hansom Cab

Postilion

A postilion guides a horse-drawn carriage while mounted on the horse or one of a pair of horses. The "driver" rides on the near horses called 'Ride Horse'. The off horse is called 'Hand Horse'. The head postilion rides on the wheel horse while the footman rides at the rear or walks. Postilions draw ceremonial vehicles on occasions of national importance. On the battlefield postilion driven allowed for better control of the horses when moving guns at high speed.

Postilion guiding a horse-drawn wagon

CLASSIFICATION OF TURNOUTS
THE HORSES/PONIES

The turnout may also be classified by the number or arrangement of horses and ponies put to the carriage. The names of the turnouts classified by horses/ponies are:

- Single
- Pair
- Tandem
- Three-abreast
- Unicorn

- Reverse Unicorn
- Four-in-Hand (Team)
- Pic-Axe
- Long Team
- Six-in-Hand

Single

One horse put to a two or four wheeled carriage. When a single horse is harnessed, it is typically between two shafts which allows it to pull evenly over long distances.

Pair

Two horses side by side - A pair of horses are typically hooked to a vehicle (usually four wheeled) with a pole between them.

Tandem

While driving tandem (one horse in front of the other) dates back to the 12th century, it first became popular as a way to reach hunts during the mid-1800s. The horse in the front (leader) is the horse that the owner would hunt with. The leader would be relatively fresh as that horse does not pull any weight, the wheeler (back horse) is actually pulling the carriage.

Tandem - short trace

Two horses: leader and wheeler with tandem bars hanging from wheeler's collar with trace tugs to wheeler traces and tandem eyes on wheeler.

Tandem - long trace (pictured at left)

Two horses: leader and wheeler
Traces are long and attached to keys on the wheeler's tug buckles.

Three abreast

There are numerous reasons to use a three-abreast configuration. In Russia, the traditional way of driving is the troika, or three-abreast, configuration. The troika is the only harness combination with different gaits of the horses. The center horse canters while the outer horses trot. This allows them to cover ground very quickly (up to 31 mph) without wearing out the horses. For much of the rest of the world, the three horses travel at a much slower pace. Three horses can pull more than two, thus making the configuration very popular with farmers.

Unicorn

The unicorn hitch is a three horse hitch, with a pair behind a single horse. The origins of the unicorn hitch are lost to history but coachmen would drive unicorn if a horse went lame and had to be left behind. Breweries sometimes used them in narrow spaces – they were easy to unhook and move a big barrel with. And then there is the farmer who trained the 'unicorn' horse to follow the cut edge of his crops, making it easier for him to watch the machinery. Regardless of the use, everyone agrees that this is a very difficult style of driving that requires a well trained leader and an experienced driver

Reverse Unicorn   *Unicorn*

Four-in-Hand (Team)

A four-in-hand is a team of four horses that are driven by a single driver. This style is used in coaching, combined driving, farming and in the show ring. Typically a horse is taught to drive single, then as a pair and then as part of a four-in-hand. The horses closest to the wheels are called wheelers and the horses farthest out are called leaders.

Long Team

A long team is made up of five horse - a four-in-hand with a cock horse. A cock horse is added to a team of horses to assist a wagon through high water or over difficult terrain. Sometimes the cock horse was ridden or kept at a point on the road where it would be needed.

Pic-Axe

A pick-axe is three horses in front of a pair..The style is native to Hungary but was also used in Spain and Australia.

Six or Eight Horse Hitch

The six and eight horse hitches are more commonly found in draft breeds as that configuration was needed to pull a heavier wagon. Stage coaches, depending on the route, were also pulled by six horse hitches as they were needed for inclines. As with four-in-hand driving the lead horses are called leaders and those closest to the vehicle are called wheelers. The team of horses in the middle are called swing horses. Wheel horses tend to be heavier as they are always pulling, swing teams need to have control and balance, while the leaders need to be confident and obedient. When making a turn the lead horses start the turn first with the rest following their lead.

Long Team

Pic-Axe

Six or Eight Horse Hitch

PARTS OF THE TURNOUT
CARRIAGES

The word carriage is from Old Northern French cariage, "to carry in a vehicle". In the US, around the end of the nineteenth century, early cars were briefly called horseless carriages. Many of the early automobile bodies were based on the body style of carriages.

Carriages may be enclosed or open, depending on the type, and they may be two-wheeled or four wheeled. A two-wheeled horse-drawn vehicle is usually called a cart. Four-wheeled vehicles have many names – one for heavy loads is most commonly called a wagon. Vehicles pulled by one horse or by horses in a single file have shafts which attach either side of the wheel horse (the rearmost horse - the one closest to the wheels). Vehicles which are pulled by a pair or by a team of several pairs have a pole which attaches between the wheel pair. Two-wheeled vehicles are balanced by the distribution of weight of the load (driver, passengers, and goods) over the axle and then held level by the animal; this means that the shafts must be fixed rigidly to the vehicle's body. Four-wheeled vehicles remain level on their own and so the shafts or pole are hinged vertically, allowing them to rise and fall with the movement of the animals. A four-wheeled vehicle is also steered by the shafts or pole, which are attached to the front axle; this swivels on a turntable or "fifth wheel" beneath the vehicle.

Many carriages are not suitable to be used in most show ring classes but may be used in Concours D'elegance classes. The listing of carriages in this section are the carriages most often seen turned out in the show ring. Some ADS shows use the type of carriage as the basis for class divisions. For example there would be class divisions for:

- Road Carts and Long Island Carts
- Runabouts
- Phaetons
- Gigs
- Miscellaneous Carriages not included in divisions above: Dog Carts, Ralli Cars, Jaunting Carts etc.
- Trade and Commercial Vehicles
- Servant Driven
- Roof-Seat Break
- Coaches

Road Cart/Sulky

- Simple two wheeled vehicle
- Sometimes seating for only one
- Usually natural wood or bright color
- Meant for road work or training or racing
- Sulkies were used for racing and are often seen in Currier and Ives prints

Ethan Allen was a Morgan horse by Black Hawk foaled June 18, 1849. Ethan Allen was the champion trotter of his time. He sired approximately seventy two foals in his lifetime, of which only two were fillies. He was featured in several Currier and Ives prints and was the model for a popular trotting horse weather vane.

Modern Road Cart

Un-restored Vintage Road Cart

Long Island Carts

- Two wheeled cart
- Meant for cross country work
- Designed to avoid bouncing out

In 1885, Charles A. Ellison of Mineola, Long Island, New York, filed a patent for a cart that would be comfortable for everyday use. With the basic concept provided by the Mineola Cart, there were several vehicles which followed – Henry M. Willis' East Williston Cart (1891), the Maplewood Cart from the catalog of J.T. Clarkson & Co (1912) and the Hempstead Cart (1900). Robert H. Nostrand's Hempstead Cart was originally advertised in The Hempstead Sentinel as 'the new Meadow Brook Cart'. The style of theses carts collectively became know as "Long Island." They rode well over rough ground, were very suitable for use by ladies and they were appropriate for business or pleasure. It has been suggested that Long Island Carts became known as Meadowbrook Carts because they were often used to follow the famous Meadowbrook Hounds (NY) through the countryside. *(cited from: https://www.carriageassociationofamerica.com/the-quirky-history-of-the-meadowbrook/)*

Meadowbrook Cart

East Williston Cart

Hempstead Cart

Runabout

- Four wheeled
- Meant for "running about" on roads
- Used for going at speed - quick and straight
- Often used as fire chief's "buggy"
- Stable at speed
- May be straight box or cut-under
- Shape of seat varies
- Some may have a rumble seat
- Popular body style for first horseless carriages

1903 Sears Runabout "Horseless Carriage"

Fire Chief's "Buggy"

Straight Box Runabout

Phaeton

- Usually more formal
- Often used for driving in the park
- May be open, covered or have a parasol
- Some phaetons were strictly daytime vehicles
- Can be used with single, pair or four-in-hand
- Cutaway body allowed for drivers and passengers to be seen in their finery
- Popular body style for first horseless carriages

George IV Phaeton

1897 Daimler Grafton Phaeton "Horseless Carriage"

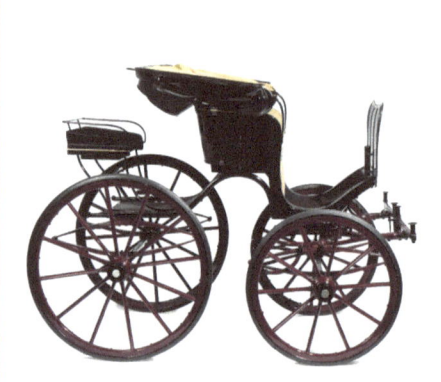

Hooded Spider Phaeton

Mail Phaeton

Wicker Phaeton

American Show Phaeton or Gooch Wagon

Gig

- Two wheeled carriage - more formal than Meadowbrook or Road Cart
- Driver's seat is higher than shafts
- Used for single horse or tandem
- Normally had two lamps with thick glass for use at night
- Often used as a vehicle for businesses purposes but also used for park driving
- Various types of springing provided a comfortable ride

Tilbury Gig

The meaning of the term 'gig' is taken from the description of a 'flighty girl' and indicates anything which whirls or is dangerous or unpredictable. Contemporary literature frequently recounted romantic tales of spills and hairbreadth scrapes from these vehicles, but is equally fulsome on the fearful thrill experienced in driving them.*(cited from: Bradney, J. (2005). The carriage-drive in Humphry Repton's landscapes. Garden History, 31-46.)*

Skeleton Gig

Stanhope gigs are named after their designer, the famous amateur driver the Honourable Fitzroy Stanhope. The Stanhope and other types of gig such as the Tilbury and Cabriolet proved to be very popular and were common sights on both town and country roads throughout the nineteenth century.

Park Gate Gig

Dennett gigs were used by gentlemen for traveling around town and country. They are always sprung on three springs, two side and one cross spring. The name 'Dennett' may have derived from the coachbuilder, Bennett, who developed the design for the gig and at some point the B became a D, or, due to the three springs, it may have been named after the Dennett sisters who were very popular at the time the springs were developed.(cited from: https://www.thecarriagefoundation.org.uk)

Miscellaneous Carriages

Going to Covert Cart

Covert – (pronounced "cover") is an area of scrub, brush, or woods where wild animals find protection. So this also is at type of carriage used for hunting.

White Chapel Cart

The Whitechapel cart is also a dog cart variant identified by the paneled sides and back. The tail board can be hinged down to act as a footboard for two passengers facing backwards, as well as the driver and passenger facing forward. All two-wheeled carriages with this arrangement need to have a sliding front seat, to adjust the balance depending on the number, position and weight of the people carried. In this case there is a crank handle which can be wound to move the front seat forwards or backwards. Bright yellow and black paintwork is typical for a sporting carriage. The Whitechapel was made popular by King Edward VII who favored this fast and versatile carriage as a smart sporting and hunting vehicle. *(cited from: https://www.thecarriagefoundation.org.uk)*

Wagonette

The Wagonette is a sporting vehicle which was popular during the late nineteenth and early twentieth centuries. They were owner driven and used for hunting as they could seat a number of people. This is a very good example and finished in the traditional varnished wood.*(cited from: https://www.thecarriagefoundation.org.uk/)*

Ralli Car

A Ralli car is a traditional type of horse-drawn cart, named after the Ralli family. The vehicle was commonly used as a general run-around for families. A true Ralli Car has shafts that run inside the body of the carriage, passing through holes in the panel at the front below the dashboard. The shape of the carriage body can vary from curved side panels incorporating the splashguards to panel sides with straight splashguards on iron brackets. The shafts tend to be fairly straight and the seating can be for two frontward facing or four back to back. They are a member of the sporting family of carriages being a variant of the Dog Cart and were used for sporting outings and running errands. Popular during the late 19th century and early 20th century. *(cited from: http://www.britishdrivingsociety.co.uk/the-ralli-car/ and https://www.thecarriagefoundation.org.uk/item/ralli-car*

Dog Cart - two wheeled

A dog cart is a general purpose two wheeled vehicle for a single horse used for transporting a gentleman, his loader, and his gun dogs, the latter being carried under the seat with side ventilation slats for their comfort. However the seating arrangement allows for four people if needed, two facing forward and two rear facing. Dog carts were also used for shopping trips, collecting a visitor from the railway station and other tasks. (cited from: http://www.britishdrivingsociety.co.uk/)

Dog Cart - four wheeled

Four wheeled Dog Carts are also popular, having seats for four persons and more room for their dogs. These may be suitable for a single when shafts are fitted, and a pair or other multiple with a pole in place. *(cited from: http://www.britishdrivingsociety.co.uk)*

Miscellaneous Carriages - Continued
Trap

Traps were country pleasure driving vehicles that were sometimes used for hunting. A small compartment in the back of the vehicle was sometimes used to house a dog, and the early traps would later become the more elaborate dog carts in America. Traps could accommodate two to four passengers and were very easy to handle. Traps often featured a rear seat that could be removed or shifted for passengers to be able to ride backwards or forwards. *(cited from: https://aaqeastend.com/contents/portfolio/long-island-museum-carriage-collection-finest-collection-of-horse-drawn-vehicles/)*

Jaunting Cart

With its origins in Ireland the Jaunting Car was a popular mode of transport that seated on average four people on back to back seats that ran lengthways with the footboards hanging over the wheels. The driver's seat was perched in between the passenger seats and quite high. They were pulled by a single horse and were often painted in bright colors and decorated. (cited from: https://www.thecarriage-foundation.org.uk)

Tub Cart

Sometimes referred to as an "inside cart" because its passengers face the interior and are protected by the closed door at the back of the vehicle. The Tub cart is a larger version of the Governess Cart, which was used by the Nanny to take small children out for their afternoon air. These larger versions were used to keep adult passengers as well as children from putting hands in the spokes of the wheels. The driver sits in the back corner of the vehicle and puts his knee in the cutout area for comfort. Passengers sit facing inward. *(cited from: https://www.thecarriagefoundation.org.uk)*

Trade and Commercial Vehicles

Let your imagination go wild! There are as many trade and commercial types of carriages as there were trades and businesses during the "horse and buggy era". Pictured here are a few that have been in the show ring.

Wayne Creamery (Detroit) milk wagon. The city made the creamery put automotive tires on the wagons to reduce noise. It was restored and repainted when Wayne Creamery became Mr. Fresh drive thru stores.

Milk Float - Champion of the Light Trade Vehicles class at the Windsor Horse Show 2012 photo by Jennifer Singleton- Carriage Association of America.

Royal Mail vehicle from the Windsor Horse Show 2012 photo by Jennifer Singleton-Carriage Association of America.

Paul Van Sickle driving Dolly an 8 year old Friesian Mare put to a 1900 oil wagon operated by the White Rose Oil Company used for home deliveries of heating oil, kerosene and gasoline.

John Greenall driving his Fishing Tackle wagon.

John Henry - "one cool mule" and his owner Kathleen Conklin driving a Butcher's Cart.

Servant Driven

Very few of these vehicles are used in classes at Carriage Driving shows due to their lack of maneuverability. They will be seen however on Pleasure Drives or in a Councours D'elegance class.

Governess Carts

Governess Carts, sometimes called Tub Carts for obvious reasons, have a deep tub-shaped body with access through a door at the back, and seats each side. They were often used by a governess (hence the name), or possibly a mother, to take the children out for a drive. She would drive sitting diagonally in the back right-hand corner. Although the seat and the cushion on the right hand side have been shaped for this purpose, this would still have been difficult and uncomfortable. Only the quietest pony, or sometimes a donkey, was suitable to be driven to a Governess Car, not only because of the awkward driving position, but because it was difficult to get out quickly and run to his head if she needed to. The cranked axle allows the body to be mounted lower, dropping the center of gravity and making it difficult to overturn. *(cited from: https://www.thecarriagefoundation.org.uk/item/governess-car-argory)*

Victoria

Victoria's were introduced by the future King Edward VII from Paris and were made popular by the patronage of Queen Victoria who favored this carriage style. Victoria's are open carriages with a leather hood to give some protection to the occupants against the sun. They were driven by a coachman with a footman sitting next to him. The low comfortable body carries two, or occasionally three if it has a folding seat stowed in the back of the boot. The low access, elegant style and comfortable seating made the Victoria very popular with ladies for fine weather use. (cited from: https://www.thecarriagefoundation.org.uk/item/panel-boot-victoria-barker)

Barouche

A carriage for taking pleasure drives in and around parks with seating for two people. The Barouches were introduced from Germany at the turn of the 19th century and were then known as German Wagons. These early barouches were heavy versatile carriages, often used for traveling as well as everyday driving. After the railways made traveling carriages redundant in the mid nineteenth century, the barouche became the ultimate park vehicle for being seen. A barouche is superficially similar to a landau but, whereas a landau has two heads which completely enclose the body, a barouche only has one, over the principal seat at the back. The front seat is covered by a knee flap, which was closed in bad weather, but could be hinged up to form a seat back for this additional seat in fine weather (cited from: https://www.thecarriagefoundation.org.uk/item/barouche)

Landau

At the start of the nineteenth century Landaus were big heavy carriages, open versions of the contemporary coaches. Later in the century, when many more people could afford to own carriages, everyday carriages became smaller and lighter. A successful professional family who could afford to employ a coachman would very likely own a brougham, a closed carriage for bad weather and night-time use, and a victoria, an open carriage for use in fine weather. This was an ideal combination but, if they owned a landau, they only needed one carriage for both uses because, with the head raised, it was a closed four seat carriage, but it could be quickly and easily converted to an open carriage simply by lowering the head. Several different styles of everyday landaus were developed. The canoe landau was obviously so named because it has a canoe-shaped body. If a canoe-bodied landau was so small that it could be pulled by one horse it was called a Sefton landau, after the Earl of Sefton for whom the first one was built, and it was considered a breakthrough for a landau to be so small at that time. If the body had an angular profile and a deep foot well it was called a Shelburne landau, after the Earl of Shelburne who had the first of that pattern built. Early landaus had head joints, the hinged stays visible outside the leather of the head, which kept it tightly stretched, but a servant had to get down to raise or lower the head. Many types of head lifts were later developed, spring-assisted mechanisms that were fitted between the head leather and the fabric head cloth 'which facilitate the closing and opening of the heads, almost as simple in action as the opening or closing of an umbrella or a parasol' as the celebrated carriage builder G. N. Hooper wrote in 1890. *(cited from: https://www.thecarriagefoundation.org.uk/item/canoe-landau-maidstone)*

The Earl of Seafield (c. 1910) is being driven with his family in a Canoe Landau put to a pair of fine carriage horses in semi-state harness. The coachman wears livery and has a footman from the household staff sitting next to him.

Roof-Seat Break

The char-à-banc was so named by French builders because the seats are placed across the carriage more or less at the same height as the driver's seat. About 1844, King Louis Philippe presented a char-à-banc to Queen Victoria. British builders copied and modified the design. Large public versions came to be built, sometimes having seats wide enough to carry four persons, and these were used for sight-seeing tours. In common parlance in Britain they were known as "sharrybangs" or "sharrers." A private char-à-banc was built with the seats almost as high as the roof seats on a coach, being mounted on a long, boxlike body. Perhaps for this reason, American builders called this sporting version a "roof-seat break." It was built in various sizes by the leading American builders and came to be used with a pair, unicorn, or a four-in-hand to take parties of friends to race-meetings or for hunting. There are many versions of Roof-Seat breaks. *(cited from: https://www.carriageassociationofamerica.com/carriage-tour/roof-seat-break-or-char-a-banc/)*

Coaches

Coaches are driven to a four-in-hand and can take eight to twelve passengers. Coaches weigh three thousand pounds and with passengers and horses the total comes to about ten thousand pounds so it is preferable to drive on a hard surface. There are several types of coaches that may be seen at Carriage Driving shows.

Road Coach

A Road Coach historically carried fare paying passengers.

*Gloria Austin
driving a Road Coach*

Private Road Coach

A Private Road Coach is driven by the owner and is made for traveling but not on a scheduled route as with the Road Coach. They are heavier than a Park Drag and have a rear seat wide enough for four passengers.

Private Drag

Private Drags were used by their owners for day trips to the races or cricket matches or drives in town or the park in order to be seen. They are lighter in construction to the Road Coach as they were not required to travel such distances or at high speed. *(cited from: https://www.thecarriagefoundation.org.uk/item/private-drag-coach)*

To learn more about coaches be sure to read the Equine Heritage book: *Coaches and Coaching Throughout the Ages* by Gloria Austin

Gloria Austin driving her Park Drag

The term Grandstand comes from sitting atop a coach. The horses would be unhitched and people would sit in the high position to see the activities of the day.

Refreshments were carried in the rear boot or in a hot food chest placed on the floor between the two interior seats.

PARTS OF THE TURNOUT
APPOINTMENTS

Carriage Toe Board or Dash Clocks and their Keys

Choosing appointments for carriages is like choosing jewelry to go with an outfit; jewelry can make or break the outfit and should not be overdone. The same can be said for carriage appointments. To some it may seem inappropriate to have lamps on a wicker, day time carriage but remember, when these carriages were ordered and made, they were made to the specifications of the owner. The general rule of thumb though on an antique is if it was not originally on the carriage, do not add it. There are many appointments available for carriages. The choice of what to use needs to be appropriate for the turnout and done tastefully. Coaches have many rules and specifications for appointments however the appointments for carriages include but are not limited to:

- Baskets for horns and umbrellas
- Spares kits for tools
- Quarter Sheet (for each horse)
- Halter and lead (for each horse)
- Slow moving vehicle sign for use where required by law
- Lamps

- Leather Dash clock with mirror, and grooming kit
- Silver Brewster & Co. Dash clock with thermometer, and powder compact
- Personal Reading Lamp

Appointments should always be placed neatly in the carriage. Here (left to right) a spares kit, halter, lead and quarter sheet are available for inspection by the judge in the back of a concord runabout.

Baskets

Baskets are appropriate on carriages such as gigs, sporting vehicles and coaches. Baskets are used to hold umbrellas, walking sticks and horns. A basket is not normally used on vehicles such as road carts, runabouts and phaetons. Baskets come in many shapes and sizes and should compliment the carriage. The basket needs to be secured well so as not to bounce around and scratch the carriage or make noise and become distracting. Placement of the basket is important too; it should be attached on the carriage where the groom or horn blower is able to easily retrieve the horn, umbrella or walking stick as needed.

Basket on back of a tandem gig along with a spare whip.

An example of various horns and basket holders for horns.

Notice the black umbrella basket on the back of Gloria Austin's Park Drag located above the rear wheel.

Spares Kit

The Spares Kit is the "emergency kit" for use if there is a breakdown while out driving. In a Turnout Class at a show the judge will often check to see if there is a Spares Kit on the carriage.

Sometimes a shoeing kit, halters, leads and quarter sheets are carried on the carriage. Food and picnic supplies are normal on a Park Drag whereas buckets, an oil can and more practical things to address a breakdown are more warranted on a Road Coach.

Spares Kits include:

- Wheel wrench (that fits the carriage!)
- Matches or lighter for lamps
- Leather punch
- Pliers
- Hammer
- Screwdriver
- Rawhide
- Rein splice
- Trace splice
- Hoofpick
- Vice grip

Leather bucket, Perfection Axle Grease Tin, Crescent Harness Oil Tin, Oil Can, Carriage Boot Key and Hinged Horse Shoe

Spares Kit from carriage Driving Essentials, Inc.

Wicker Baskets with picnic and tea supplies.

Lamps

There were no lanterns or lamps bright enough to illuminate the roadway prior to the invention of carbide lamps in the 1900s. Lamps were used on carriages not for illuminating the road, but for visibility; carriages needed to be seen by approaching riders and carriages. Lamps on carriages also became a status symbol as some were quite ornate and costly.

There are many styles and patterns of lamps and often times, when an antique carriage is purchased, the original lamps are not on the carriage. Keep in mind too that when carriages were originally used people put what they liked or wanted on a carriage; there were no "show rules" or specifications designated what should be used. Generally though lamp choice will follow some general guidelines:

- Small lamps with round front glass are generally used on two wheel carts and gigs.
- Cylinder lamps often are used on Broughams, Landaus and large vehicles.
- Horizontal cylinder (mail) lamps and square lamps with round, oval or horseshoe shaped flanges are most frequently found on sporting carriages.
- Basic square lamps will compliment most vehicles.

Various lamp styles

Gloria Austin giving a presentation on Carriage Lamps.

To learn more about lamps be sure to read the Equine Heritage book: *Carriage Lamps* by: Gloria Austin

Lamp on a Gig

Lamp on a Phaeton

Lamp on a Gala State Carriage

PARTS OF THE TURNOUT
THE PEOPLE

The Whip (Driver)

The Whip could be a Lady, a Gentleman or a Junior Driver. No matter who is driving, the following items are essential:

- Hat (protective headgear for junior drivers)
- Gloves
- Lap Robe/Apron
- Whip

Hat

Some people consider selecting the hat the most enjoyable part of putting the turnout together. The hat can also detract from the turnout so there are a few things to keep in mind when selecting a hat:

- The hat should be worn so that the brim is parallel to the ground.
- It should fit snug to prevent blowing off in the wind.
- The style should be appropriate to the carriage - formal or informal.
- The size should be appropriate to carriage size. (Ladies - the bigger the carriage, the bigger the hat!)
- The color should coordinate with the lady's attire.
- The hat needs to be seasonally appropriate - straw for summer felt for fall or winter.
- The style of a lady's hat is also important - brim for daytime, brimless for evening.

Felt hat for fall/winter

Straw hat for summer

A popular summer hat for a man is the straw boater as it goes with most turn-outs. A cap or Fedora will also work with most carriages. A derby or bowler is more formal, but not everyone looks good in one. If the vehicle is formal, then a gray topper during the day is ideal for driver and passengers. Grooms wear black toppers. *(cited from: http://users.vermontel.net/~greenall/documents/*

Boater

Derby

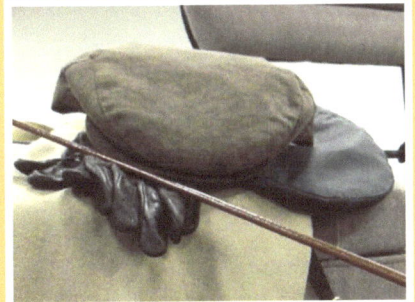
Cap

Gray Top Hat

Men's Leather Hat Box

Lady's Fifth Avenue Hat Box

Felt hat for fall or winter

The bigger the carriage, the bigger the hat

A smaller hat for a smaller carriage

Brimless hat for evening

Gloves

The purpose of gloves is to protect your hands. There are a few things to keep in mind when selecting gloves:

- Since reins are brown leather, it looks best if gloves are brown leather too. Using brown gloves also prevents dye from coming off the gloves onto the reins.
- Gloves should be reinforced in the proper place for driving.
- White knit rain gloves may be placed handily under the driver's seat.

Brown gloves

Note the white knit rain gloves tucked under the driver's seat for use when needed.

Lap Robe/Apron

The driver and passengers of vehicles wear a lap robe or apron. The apron should wrap completely around the body and cover the body from about four inches above the waist to mid-shin bone. Passengers may use a lap robe which is large piece of material about three to four feet square that covers everyone on the seat. These robes and aprons should be of a color which harmonizes with the material of the seat. They can be solid color, checks or plaid and are made of a fabric that is a seasonably appropriate weight and color. It is sometimes advisable, when having a lap robe or apron made, to make it reversible, thus going with the upholstery of different vehicles. It is also correct to edge the apron and lap robe with the color matching the striping of the carriage. Monograms add a nice touch. The lap robe is an appointment of the carriage so it is left on/with the carriage when the driver or passenger get off of the carriage.
(cited from: http://users.vermontel.net/~greenall/documents/appointmentsfordrivingantiquecarriages.pdf)

Lap robes

Lap robes

Whip

The driver MUST have a whip and they MUST carry it. The whip is used for signaling, saluting and directing the horse. This is why the reins are carried in the left hand. The whip is moved to the left hand when operating the brake.

The whip

- should have a thong long enough to reach the front shoulder of the lead horse.
- should be tan color.
- is preferably made of holly or other wood with white lash and drab colored popper.
- stick and thong length should be appropriate to the turnout – single, pair, tandem or four-in-hand.
- can be a bow, drop thong or buggy whip.

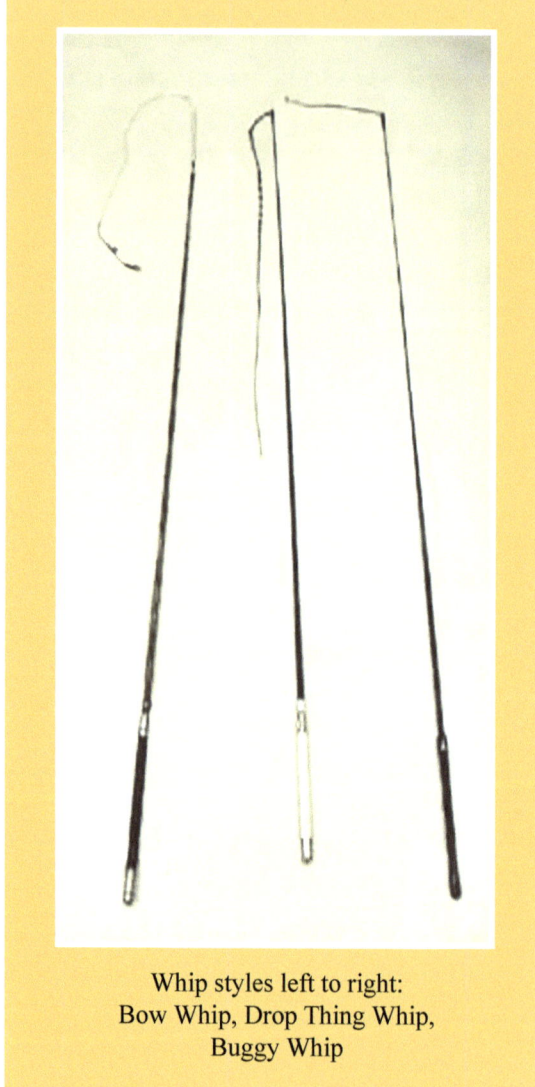

Whip styles left to right:
Bow Whip, Drop Thing Whip,
Buggy Whip

The whip is used for signaling and saluting.

Left Turn

Right Turn

Stop

Lady's Vertical Salute

Lady's Horizontal Salute

Gentleman's Salute
Whip - in left hand
Hat - right side up and to the side.
Prince Phillip and his coachman
David E. Saunders

The Coachman And Grooms

The groom needs to be able to be identified and ready to work as needed. The livery ('uniform') worn by grooms is functional and considered to be 'traditional', not a 'costume'. The number of grooms varies depending on the turnout. Four-in-hand and unicorn turnouts require two grooms. Pair, Tandem and VSE four-in-hand and unicorn turnouts require one groom. A groom is optional for a single horse or pony turnout. Today many four-in-hands are driven by the owner and the coachman dresses as a passenger with a black top hat; the coachman may sit in front and take the reins if needed or may sit behind the driver and control the brake. Traditionally, the coachman's first concern was to be the driver and to remain in full control of the horses. Another employee, traditionally a footman, would accompany the coach to handle any circumstances beyond the coachman's control.

Livery may be either:
- Full (Formal)
- Stable

Stable/Informal Livery can be casual or more formal. A more formal type of stable livery would consist of a suit, white shirt, dark tie, derby, dark shoes and brown leather gloves. Casual stable livery would consist of a hunting/hacking jacket, stock tie and pin, derby, jodhpurs without reinforcements, brown paddock boots and brown leather gloves. Another option for casual stable livery would be a conservative sport coat, dark tie, derby or cap, tan trousers, brown paddock boots and brown leather gloves.

If a woman is the groom, she should have little or no makeup, no earrings and hair should be neatly in a net.

Stable Livery

Full/Formal Livery is a black coat or a coat in the family/farm color with five, four, two or even no buttons on the cuffs. The coachman or senior groom have four buttons at the back of their coats and six buttons at the front of their coats. The junior groom has six buttons at the back of the coat and five buttons at the front of the coat With a team of four, when the carriage is stationary, the coachman or senior groom stands with the wheelers and the junior groom stands at the heads of the leaders. The coachman (when in livery) and grooms wear white breeches. The breeches do not have the reinforcements as for riding. Both wear black boots with tan tops and a Newmarket tie or stock with tan or natural leather gloves. A black top hat should be worn with only staff or commission officers, diplomatic corps and nobility entitled to wear cockades.

Formal Livery

The Guard

The guard, a vestige of the Mail Coach, protected the cargo and passengers from the highwaymen who would steal valuables from passengers and take unprotected cargo. The guard was the master of the ship in that he kept the time with a clock in the front of his pouch and he also carried the weigh bills inside the pouch. The key to the boot could be found on the front of the pouch so he could easily access the mail and parcels carried on board. The scarlet uniform was a tradition in Great Britain, with white breeches and leggings over his paddock boots, he was a majestic figure atop the coach. The Guard today on a Road Coach wears the same uniform.

James Nobbs, the last mail coach guard.

Guard Livery with Pouch

The Horn Sounder

The job of the horn sounder is to...sound the horn! The powerful noise of a horn was the best way to get their messages across: There were tunes for 'clear the road', 'off side', 'near side', 'slacken the pace' and so on. Many farms and owners also had their own tunes to announce their arrival. Gloria Austin's tune, "Twig, Tweet and Trot" was written for her by The Canadian Tootlers. In the days of the Mail Coaches, the Guard was the horn sounder. Today, the horn sounder may be the Guard, if the coach is a Road Coach, otherwise, the horn sounder should be dressed conservatively in a suit and a derby/bowler.

"Twig, Tweet and Trot" written for Gloria by The Canadian Tootlers.

Gloria Austin driving at Windsor Castle for the Queen's 90th birthday with Horn Sounder, Ray Tuckwiller.

The Passengers

Passengers should wear conservative, contemporary attire including gloves, hat and a lap robe. Sunglasses should be avoided for the passengers as well as the whip and grooms. Where grooms or passengers are required by ADS rules, they must be closely available and capable of rendering assistance at all times. Grooms or passengers are not allowed to leave their respective positions on the vehicle while it is in motion or attempt to correct a problem without first being put down. When a groom or passenger is put down to head the horse or horses during a line-up, he or she must remount when the driver moves off.

Everyone should always be prepared for inclement weather. The whip should have white knit gloves. If there is an umbrella basket - it should have umbrellas.

The Dog

Some Carriage Driving Shows have classes for a dog to participate and be judged. The dog is judged primarily on suitability of the dog to serve as a companion while the turnout shows both ways in the arena at a walk, slow trot and working trot. The dog may be standing, lying down or seated on the vehicle or may run behind, beside or at the axle of the vehicle. The dog must be under control at all times and can not be led on the ground from the vehicle or be restrained by being tied to the vehicle, driver or passenger. Most importantly, the dog should not interfere with the driver in any way.

As you can imagine, this is a hard class for the judge to place! Often spectators, in the form of applause, may judge this class. The judge stands behind each entry and raises a hand, asking the spectators to respond.

American Driving Society Rules For Attire

If you plan to show, you should be aware of the ADS rules/requirements for attire.

1. Formal Or Park
(Park Drag, Road Coach, Breaks, Mail Stanhope, Demi-Mail, Spider Phaeton, Stanhope or Park Gate Gig, George IV, Basket Phaeton, etc.)
a. Gentlemen to wear gloves, a top hat or bowler, suit jacket and tie. If the class is in the evening, gentlemen may choose to wear white or black tie.
b. Ladies to wear gloves, a stylish hat that may have a veil, long sleeved dress or blouse suitable for a formal affair. If the class is in the evening, ladies may opt not to wear a hat and may wear a formal gown.
c. Brown gloves are always appropriate for the driver unless rain gloves are needed.
d. Apron or lap robe should be of a solid color material and harmonize with the upholstery (in warmer weather tattersall or checked aprons are appropriate for day classes).
e. Period costumes are not to be used, and conservative dress appropriate to the style of the vehicle is encouraged.

2. Sporting Vehicles
Breaks, Four-Wheeled Dog Carts, Traps, Tandem Gig, Saylor Wagon, etc.)
a. Gentlemen to wear gloves, a bowler, boater, fedora, straw hat or cap, a suit or sport jacket and tie.
b. Ladies to wear gloves, a felt or straw hat (no veil), long-sleeved dress or blouse suitable for a country outing.
c. Brown gloves are always appropriate for the driver.
d. Attendants to wear stable livery defined as:
(i) Conservative suit, dark tie, derby, dark shoes and leather gloves.
(ii) Conservative jacket, jodhpurs or drill trousers, jodhpur boots or paddock boots, white shirt, stock or four-in-hand tie, derby or conservative cap and leather gloves.
(iii) Hunting attire with a hunting derby or bowler and leather gloves.
e. Aprons may be of solid, checked or plaid material.
f. There are occasions when it may be appropriate for the driver to turn out more formally.

3. Informal Or Country
(Village Cart, Two-Wheeled Dog Cart, Road or Jogging Cart, Four-Wheeled Buggy, Runabout, American Stanhope, Bronson Wagon, Surrey, Rockaway, etc.)
Attire and livery are the same as with a sporting vehicle.

4. Commercial
Attire should be traditionally correct for the type of commercial turnout
(cited from: https://americandrivingsociety.org/Portals/ADS/2-8-20%20Redline%20book.pdf)

PARTS OF THE TURNOUT
THE HARNESS

The harness should fit the horse(s) well, be clean and in good condition.

When looking at a turnout the harness should not detract from the overall turnout; it should just blend in and fit the horse and carriage properly in order to be functional. No part of the harness should be pinching the horse nor should it be so loose as to not be effective or worse yet, unsafe. The traces should not be hanging and the breeching should not be drooping or too high. If using a full collar, it should fit without bouncing or pinching. The bridle should fit well with the eye of the horse in the center of the blinker and the cavesson properly adjusted.

Black harness is considered appropriate with painted vehicles, with shaft and pole trimmings done in black. It is also considered appropriate with a natural wood vehicle with iron parts painted any color except brown. When using black harness shaft and pole trimmings, dash and fenders are done in black.

Russet (brown) harness is considered appropriate with natural wood vehicles with brown or black iron, a painted vehicle with natural wood panels with any color iron or a vehicle that is painted brown with brown iron. Shaft and pole trimmings should match the harness and therefore be russet as well.

Black harness

Bridles should fit snugly to prevent catching on the vehicle or other pieces of harness. A throatlatch and a full nose-band or cavesson are mandatory.

Brown harness

All of the metal furnishings on a harness should match, be secure and polished.

Breast collars are appropriate with lightweight vehicles. Full collars are suggested for heavy vehicles such as coaches, breaks, phaetons, gigs, dog carts, etc.

Breast collars

Full collars

A correctly-fitting harness saddle is important for the comfort of the horse. A wide saddle is suggested for two-wheeled vehicles, as more weight rests on the horse's back. Narrower saddles are more appropriate for four-wheeled vehicles.

Wide saddle

Narrow saddle

In the show ring, the ADS recognizes specific national types of harness.

Hungarian harness with cut "Sallangs". 1880-90

PARTS OF THE TURNOUT
THE HORSE

The driving horse must be serviceably sound and may be of any breed, color or size so long as it is capable of performing the required gaits. The tot is the gait of the driving horse since it is most effective for sustainable distance travel. In the show ring the horse will be asked to perform a slow trot, working trot and strong trot. The horse must also walk, back, halt and stand quietly.

The horse should be well groomed,. Braiding of the mane is optional. Any mane, tail or fetlock trimming may conform to breed standards. Tails are not braided.

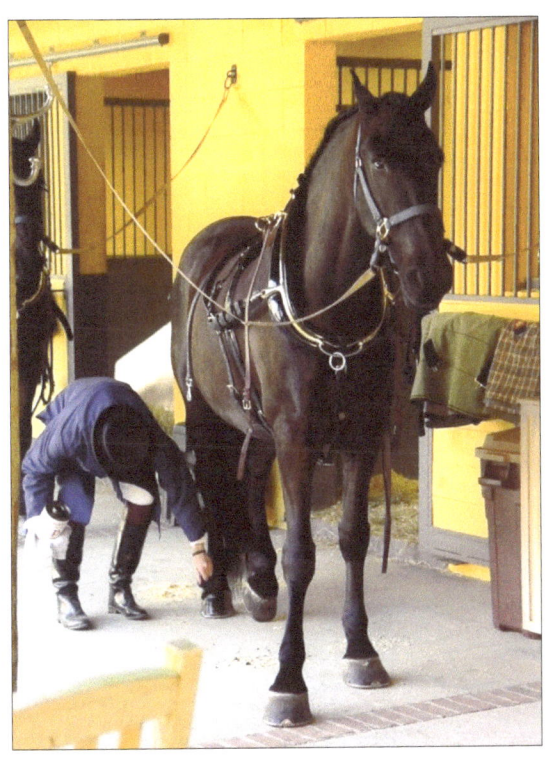

PUTTING IT ALL TOGETHER

On the next pages there are turnouts of every imaginable type. Try your luck at naming the type of carriage. (The answers are at the end of the section.) Then, using all of the knowledge you have gained reading this book so far, you can also decide what you like about each turnout and what, if anything, you might change.

Some things about a turnout are indeed personal preference and some things are "rules". If you plan to show, you should know the ADS rules/requirements for turnouts which are listed at the end of this section after all of the turnout pictures.

#1 Type of Carriage_____

What I like_____
_____
_____
_____
_____
_____

What I would change _____
_____
_____
_____
_____
_____

#2 Type of Carriage_____

What I like_____
_____
_____
_____
_____
_____

What I would change _____
_____
_____
_____
_____
_____

#3 Type of Carriage_____

What I like_____
_____
_____
_____
_____
_____

What I would change _____
_____
_____
_____
_____
_____

#4 Type of Carriage_____

What I like_____
_____
_____
_____
_____
_____

What I would change _____
_____
_____
_____
_____
_____
_____

#5 Type of Carriage_____

What I like_____
_____
_____
_____
_____
_____

What I would change _____
_____
_____
_____
_____
_____

#6 Type of Carriage _____

What I like _____
_____
_____
_____
_____
_____
_____

What I would change _____
_____
_____
_____
_____
_____
_____
_____

#7 Type of Carriage_____

What I like_____
_____
_____
_____
_____
_____

What I would change _____
_____
_____
_____
_____
_____
_____

#8 Type of Carriage_____

What I like_____
_____
_____
_____
_____
_____

What I would change _____
_____
_____
_____
_____
_____
_____

#9 Type of Carriage_____

What I like_____
_____
_____
_____
_____
_____

What I would change _____
_____
_____
_____
_____
_____
_____

#10 Type of Carriage_____

What I like_____
_____
_____
_____
_____
_____

What I would change _____
_____
_____
_____
_____
_____
_____

#11 Type of Carriage_____

What I like_____
_____
_____
_____
_____
_____

What I would change _____
_____
_____
_____
_____
_____

#12 Type of Carriage_____

What I like_____
_____
_____
_____
_____
_____

What I would change _____
_____
_____
_____
_____
_____

#13 Type of Carriage_____

What I like_____
_____
_____
_____
_____
_____

What I would change _____
_____
_____
_____
_____
_____
_____

#14 Type of Carriage_____

What I like_____
_____
_____
_____
_____
_____

What I would change _____
_____
_____
_____
_____
_____
_____

#15 Type of Carriage_____

What I like_____
_____
_____
_____
_____
_____

What I would change _____
_____
_____
_____
_____
_____
_____

#16 Type of Carriage_____

What I like_____
_____
_____
_____
_____
_____

What I would change _____
_____
_____
_____
_____
_____
_____

#17 Type of Carriage_____

What I like_____
_____
_____
_____
_____
_____

What I would change _____
_____
_____
_____
_____
_____

#18 Type of Carriage_____

What I like_____
_____
_____
_____
_____
_____

What I would change _____
_____
_____
_____
_____
_____

#19 Type of Carriage_____

What I like_____
_____
_____
_____
_____
_____

What I would change _____
_____
_____
_____
_____
_____

#20 Type of Carriage_____

What I like_____
_____
_____
_____
_____
_____

What I would change _____
_____
_____
_____
_____
_____

#21 Type of Carriage_____

What I like_____
_____
_____
_____
_____
_____

What I would change _____
_____
_____
_____
_____
_____
_____

#22 Type of Carriage_____

What I like_____
_____
_____
_____
_____
_____

What I would change _____
_____
_____
_____
_____
_____
_____

#23 Type of Carriage _____

What I like _____
_____
_____
_____
_____
_____

What I would change _____
_____
_____
_____
_____
_____

#24 Type of Carriage _____

What I like _____
_____
_____
_____
_____
_____

What I would change _____
_____
_____
_____
_____
_____

#25 Type of Carriage _____

What I like _____
_____
_____
_____
_____
_____

What I would change _____
_____
_____
_____
_____
_____

#26 Type of Carriage _____

What I like _____
_____
_____
_____
_____
_____

What I would change _____
_____
_____
_____
_____
_____

#27 Type of Carriage_____

What I like_____
_____
_____
_____
_____
_____

What I would change _____
_____
_____
_____
_____
_____
_____

#28 Type of Carriage_____

What I like_____
_____
_____
_____
_____
_____

What I would change _____
_____
_____
_____
_____
_____
_____

#29 Type of Carriage_____

What I like_____
_____
_____
_____
_____
_____

What I would change _____
_____
_____
_____
_____
_____
_____

#30 Type of Carriage_____

What I like_____
_____
_____
_____
_____
_____

What I would change _____
_____
_____
_____
_____
_____
_____

#31 Type of Carriage_____

What I like_____
_____
_____
_____
_____
_____

What I would change _____
_____
_____
_____
_____
_____

#32 Type of Carriage_____

What I like_____
_____
_____
_____
_____
_____

What I would change _____
_____
_____
_____
_____
_____

#33 Type of Carriage _____

What I like _____
_____
_____
_____
_____
_____

What I would change _____
_____
_____
_____
_____
_____

#34 Type of Carriage _____

What I like _____
_____
_____
_____
_____
_____

What I would change _____
_____
_____
_____
_____
_____

#35 Type of Carriage_____

What I like_____
_____
_____
_____
_____
_____

What I would change _____
_____
_____
_____
_____
_____
_____

#36 Type of Carriage_____

What I like_____
_____
_____
_____
_____
_____

What I would change _____
_____
_____
_____
_____
_____
_____

#37 Type of Carriage _____

What I like _____
_____
_____
_____
_____
_____

What I would change _____
_____
_____
_____
_____
_____

#38 Type of Carriage _____

What I like _____
_____
_____
_____
_____
_____

What I would change _____
_____
_____
_____
_____
_____

#39 Type of Carriage_____

What I like_____
_____
_____
_____
_____
_____

What I would change _____
_____
_____
_____
_____
_____
_____

#40 Type of Carriage_____

What I like_____
_____
_____
_____
_____
_____

What I would change _____
_____
_____
_____
_____
_____
_____

#41 Type of Carriage_____

What I like_____
_____
_____
_____
_____
_____

What I would change _____
_____
_____
_____
_____
_____

#42 Type of Carriage_____

What I like_____
_____
_____
_____
_____
_____

What I would change _____
_____
_____
_____
_____
_____

#43 Type of Carriage_____

What I like_____
_____
_____
_____
_____

What I would change _____
_____
_____
_____
_____
_____

#44 Type of Carriage_____

What I like_____
_____
_____
_____
_____

What I would change _____
_____
_____
_____
_____
_____

#45 Type of Carriage_____

What I like_____
_____
_____
_____
_____
_____

What I would change _____
_____
_____
_____
_____
_____
_____

#46 Type of Carriage_____

What I like_____
_____
_____
_____
_____
_____

What I would change _____
_____
_____
_____
_____
_____
_____

#47 Type of Carriage _____

What I like _____
_____
_____
_____
_____
_____

What I would change _____
_____
_____
_____
_____
_____

#48 Type of Carriage _____

What I like _____
_____
_____
_____
_____
_____

What I would change _____
_____
_____
_____
_____
_____

#49 Type of Carriage _____

What I like _____
_____
_____
_____
_____
_____

What I would change _____
_____
_____
_____
_____
_____

#50 Type of Carriage _____

What I like _____
_____
_____
_____
_____
_____

What I would change _____
_____
_____
_____
_____
_____

#51 Type of Carriage _____

What I like _____
_____
_____
_____
_____

What I would change _____
_____
_____
_____
_____
_____

#52 Type of Carriage _____

What I like _____
_____
_____
_____
_____

What I would change _____
_____
_____
_____
_____
_____

#53 Type of Carriage_____

What I like_____
_____
_____
_____
_____
_____

What I would change _____
_____
_____
_____
_____
_____

#54 Type of Carriage_____

What I like_____
_____
_____
_____
_____
_____

What I would change _____
_____
_____
_____
_____
_____

#55 Type of Carriage_____

What I like_____
_____
_____
_____
_____
_____

What I would change _____
_____
_____
_____
_____
_____
_____

#56 Type of Carriage_____

What I like_____
_____
_____
_____
_____
_____

What I would change _____
_____
_____
_____
_____
_____
_____

Carriage Identification From Pages 58-86

1	Spider Phaeton	35	Back to Back Dog Cart
2	Road Cart	36	Spider Phaeton
3	Cocking Cart	37	Vis-à-vis
4	Concord Wagon	38	Tandem Gig
5	Ice Wagon (Commercial Vehicle)	39	Slat Side Phaeton
6	Landau – Postilion	40	Gig
7	Demi-Mail Phaeton	41	Back to Back Trap
8	Meadowbrook Cart	42	Gig
9	Runabout	43	Wicker Phaeton
10	Roof Seat Break	44	"Flyer" newly made CDE type vehicle
11	Park Drag	45	Road Cart
12	Road Cart	46	Shooting Break
13	Wicker Phaeton	47	Back to Back Trap
14	Bronson Wagon	48	Utility CDE type vehicle
15	Park Drag	49	Wicker Phaeton
16	Dog Cart	50	Runabout
17	Road Coach	51	Gig
18	Road Cart	52	Presentation vehicle for CDE competition
19	Concord Wagon	53	Phaeton
20	Governess Cart	54	Slat Side Trap
21	Phaeton Body Road Cart	55	George IV Phaeton
22	Private Road Coach	56	Dog Cart
23	"Flyer" newly made CDE type vehicle with added wicker		
24	Wicker Phaeton		
25	Phaeton		
26	Road Cart		
27	Dog Cart/Trap		
28	Gig		
29	Phaeton		
30	Spindle Seat Road Cart		
31	Village Cart		
32	Phaeton		
33	Gig		
34	Road Cart		

AMERICAN DRIVING SOCIETY
RULES FOR TURNOUTS

1. PARK DRAG OR PRIVATE COACH

Definition: A Park Drag should be of less heavy build than a Road Coach. The axles may be Mail or Collinges. The hind seat should be mounted on curved iron braces and be of the proper width for two grooms. The lazy-backs on the roof seats should be hinged and turned down when not in use. The door of the hind boot is often hinged at the bottom so that it may be used as a serving table when open. There should be no luggage rails or straps between the seats. The driver may choose to have passengers on the Drag or Coach during coaching classes.

Paint and bodywork: The paintwork should be well finished in traditional style. The sides of the front and rear boots, the upper quarters of the body, the steps and seat rails should be painted black. The under-carriage, the pole, the bars, the underside of the footboard and the seat-risers or cheeks should be painted the same color; the lower panels of the body and the

door of the rear boot may be painted the same or a different color. An heraldic badge or monogram may be neatly painted on the crest panel of the door, on the rear boot door or on the underside of the footboard. The outside seats may be trimmed in pigskin or wool broadcloth of a suitable color with the underside of the cushions covered in waterproof material. The inside of the coach may be trimmed in Morocco leather or cloth or a combination of these materials. The inside floor may be covered with a Wilton carpet of solid color. It is not usual to have seatfalls to the outside seats, but they may be fitted inside. The seat valances or borders of the outside seats may be made of patent leather fastened with a horizontal strip of bright metal beading of the same metal as the door handles and lock covers. The metal edging to the doors and hind boot should not be polished, but there should be bright metal on the seat edge beading, door handles, and outer face of the hub caps. The glasses of the door windows should be plain and not quartered.

Appointments: There may be wine coolers and a glass case carried in the rear boot. A lunch chest or imperial may be carried on the roof but only when it is to be used as at a race meeting or similar occasion. Two spare lead bars, one side and one main, should be carried, and fastened to the back of the hind seat, with the main bar above. A folding iron ladder should be carried on brackets beneath the hind seat. The stick and umbrella basket is hung on the near-side, at the corner of the rear roof-seat, the drag shoe and safety hook should be hung under the coach on the off-side except in countries where they drive on the left of the road, in which case the drag is hung on the near-side. A spare jointed whip mounted on a board may be hung under the box-seat or inside the coach. The lamps should not be in their brackets in daylight hours, but carried in special fittings inside the coach. The window or stable shutters should be down and the windows in place when the owner or his representative is driving. The coachman's apron when not in use should be folded outside out and laid on the driving cushion. Passengers' knee rugs or lap-robes should be folded and laid on the front inside seat when not in use.

Spares: Spares may be carried in the rear boot or inside the coach. The usual includes a small case of tools comprised of wrench, hammer, leather punch screw driver, hoof pick, spare shoe and nails or "easy boot," spare lead and wheel trace, spare lead and wheel rein or rein splicer, spare hame strap, length of strong cord or wire. Loin or quarter rugs for the horses and halters should be carried in a convenient place.

Harness: The harness should be of black leather with patent leather where appropriate. The hames should have solid draft eyes and kidney links with kidney link rings on the wheelers only. Bearing reins are permitted but should be on all the horses or none. A neat monogram or badge is permitted on the winkers, drops, pads, breast-plate drops, and rosettes. The breastplates should be fastened round the collar as well as the kidney links for preference. Collars are not to be tied together. It is suggested that reins should be held in one hand, the other hand being able to assist as required. The wheel traces should have metal loop ends or quick-release. The lead traces should be put on with screw heads of the cock-eyes uppermost, as also should be the lead-bar screws. Buxton bits are preferred, and if bearing reins are used they should be on all horses and be attached to separate bearing rein bits, not to the driving bit. Cruppers may be sewn or buckled on. The reins should be made of single brown leather. Appropriate straps should be lined and stitched. The bridles may have metal browbands on fronts, or they may be of other material to match the color of the coach. Hame straps should be put on with the points inside. The metal furniture of the harness should be of the same metal as the buttons of the grooms' coats and the door handles and beading of the coach. West End buckles are preferred. The pole chains, the pole-head and the lead-bar hooks and mountings should be made of bright steel color. The pole chains may have spring hooks at each end or may have open hooks with rubber securing rings at one end. Preferably the chains should be of a length that admits the snapping of both hooks into the pole-head ring. If too short, one end should be hooked into the pole-head ring and the other into a link with the snap down. If too long, one end should be snapped in the pole-head ring, snap down, and the other brought through that ring and snapped in a link at the appropriate length.

Attendants: Two grooms in Livery should sit on the rear seat when the coach is moving, the senior groom on the right. When the coach is stopped, the senior groom stands by the right wheeler, able to take instructions from the driver, while the other groom stands at the leaders' heads.

Horses: Park Drag horses should be perfectly matched as to color, size, style, action and temperament. They should be horses of quality but with sufficient substance to handle a loaded coach. Flashy coloring is not appropriate. They should have good manners, and should be capable of moving at a stylish trot with action but not excessively fast. They should stand quietly and move off together at a walk when asked to do so.

2. ROAD COACH

Definition: A Road Coach is of stronger build than a Park Drag. The Coach may be finished as a Public or Private Road Coach, the latter carries no place names. The axles may be Mail or Collinges. The hind seat holds three persons besides the guard whose seat is on the near-side with an extra cushion. The lazy backs of the seats are usually not hinged. He should have a hand strap to take hold of when standing to sound the horn. There is a rail and luggage straps between the seats. The door of the rear boot is usually hinged on the off-side.

Paint and bodywork: The distribution of black and color in the paintwork follows the same pattern as a Park Drag, but the colors may be brighter. A Road Coach may have an appropriate name painted on the panel below the hind seat; a figure or some device associated with the coach name may be painted on side and hind boot door panels. The names of places on the coach's route may be painted on the sides. If the wheels and other parts of the undercarriage are striped, it should be with a single broad stripe. The windows are usually quartered and the coach is driven with the stable shutters down. The outside seats may be trimmed in strong material such as coach carpet or Bedford cord, not leather. The inside of the coach is usually paneled in hardwood with seat cushions of drab cloth. The seat valances may be similar to the Park Drag or may be made of wood. The metal trim is similar to the Park Drag, except that the pole-head, lead bar hooks and pole-chains may be painted black and not of bright steel.

Appointments: Two spare lead-bars, one side and one main, should be carried, fastened to the back of the hind seat with the main bar above. The folding ladder which may be made of wood is hung on brackets below the rear boot. The side lamps should be in their brackets, ready for use, and a red rear light may be placed on a bracket below the rear seat on the nearside. It is usual for this lamp to have a clear lens on the right side so that it can illuminate inside the boot when the door is open. The stick and umbrella basket is hung on the near side at the corner of the rear roof-seat. The drag-shoe and safety hook should be hung under the coach on the off side. A spare jointed whip mounted on a board may be hung under the box seat or inside the coach. The coachman's driving apron and the passenger's rugs are carried also. Inside the coach there are leather pockets on the doors and leather hat straps on the roof.

Spares: These are the same as for the Park Drag and Private Coach, but the Road Coach may also carry a canvas bucket. Halters and loin or quarter rugs for the horses should be carried in a convenient place.

Harness: The hardware of the harness should be of the same metal as the fittings of the coach. The harness is of black leather with most straps of single (unlined) leather. Collars may be of plain black or brown leather. Collars are not to be tied together. It is suggested that reins should be held in one hand, the other hand being able to assist as required. The hames should be of ring-draft type with short kidney links, chain and hook. Bearing reins are not usual but may be used on one or more horses if really necessary. The harness may be embellished with some symbolic device or the initial of the coach's name on the winkers, rosettes and pads. The wheel traces may have quick-release or French loop ends, and more rarely chain trace ends are used.

Attendants: A Road Coach carries a guard who is usually dressed in a frock coat of appropriate color, usually with strappings across the front and on the pocket flaps, breeches which may be white or of sponge-bag check, leather or canvas leggings, brown boots and a beaver hat. He carries a way-bill pouch slung over the shoulder with a pocket for a watch and a loop for the hind-boot key. He sits on the near side of the hind seat and his seat carries an extra cushion. He should have a hand strap to take hold of when standing to sound the horn. A groom in stable livery must also be carried.

Horses: Road Coach horses should be matched for size, weight, action and temperament, and way of going. They need not be matched perfectly for color and flashy markings are not objectionable. They should be of sufficient weight to be able to pull the coach without appearing to labor at all. Although the wheelers may be the stronger horses, all the horses should be capable of working in the wheel. The horses should work evenly together all the time and be capable of moving at a good pace. They should stand quietly and move off together at the walk. It is acceptable for a Road Coach team to have a gray near leader. Tradition holds that the color would be more easily seen by oncoming traffic in the dark.

3. FOUR-IN-HAND BREAKS

Definition: The Body or Wagonette Break, the Roof-Seat Break and an Omnibus with a roof-seat are vehicles in this category. All are classed as sporting vehicles.

Paint and bodywork: The underside of the footboard, the rear boot door and the front seat risers may be painted in the same color. The remainder of the body is usually painted black but the undercarriage may be painted in some bright color. The seat cushions can be trimmed in Bedford cord, corduroy, leather or broadcloth. Seat falls are not usual. A stick basket, ladder if needed, spare bars and a spare jointed whip are carried. The side lamps are usually left in place ready for use.

Spares: Spares and other equipment are carried as for a coach, and these are usually stowed in the rear boot.

Harness: The harness is of a fairly simple kind without unnecessary embellishments. Breechings may be used on the wheelers if they are likely to be required. The wheel traces may have metal loops, French loops or quick-release ends. The hames may be solid draft with kidney links or ring-draft with short kidney links, chains and hooks. Liverpool or elbow bits are appropriate, except in formal occasions, with grooms in livery, when Buxton bits could be used.

Appointments: Sporting breaks are usually turned out informally with the driver wearing country clothes and a bowler hat, the grooms in stable livery of trousers, jacket, shirt and tie with a bowler hat. However there are occasions when it may be appropriate for the driver to turn out more formally with a top hat and driving coat. The grooms could then wear livery. In such a case Buxton bits could be used.

Horses: The horses for a sporting break should be matched as to type and action. If they are matched as to color, or "cross-matched," that is diagonally matched as to color, so much the better. They should move well together, be capable of a sustained active walk and a smart trot. They can be expected to rein back readily and to stand quietly. They should move off quietly and together, starting at a walk until asked to trot.

4. MAIL, STANHOPE, DEMI-MAIL, SPIDER, GEORGE IV PHAETONS

Definition: These vehicles are intended to be driven by the owner or a friend and are usually turned out in the more formal "park" style rather than in country style.

Paint and bodywork: In all cases the body is painted black, except for the seat panel which may be finished in imitation cane or in a color to match or blend with the color of the undercarriage. The undercarriage may be painted in an appropriate bright color and striped. The cushions may be covered in dark-colored broadcloth with the seat back upholstered in black leather or, in the case of a Spider Phaeton without a top, in black patent leather. There may be a loose floor mat of heavy punched rubber over a floor covered with linoleum, or ribbed rubber may be laid on the floor boards. If there is a folding top, the valance may be of patent leather pinned in place with polished metal beading. The dash may have a folded waterproof apron attached or have leather loops for securing such an apron. A whip socket is usual. Lamps are of round dial pattern in most cases but show Spider Phaetons usually have square pattern lamps.

Spares: A small kit of tools, a wheel wrench and spare harness parts should be carried.

Appointments: A dashboard clock and waterproof coats are necessary.

Harness: When it is possible to use a single horse with phaetons of this class, the harness has a bridle of square or D-shaped winkers; browband and rosettes of metal; Buxton bit; sidecheck bearing rein if any; Kay collar and hames with chain and ring coupling at the bottom; back-strap lined and stitched with crupper stitched on; breastplate; saddle of English pattern, 4 or 4-1/2 inches wide with French or Tilbury tugs, reins of brown leather. Pair harness is similar in character with solid-draft hames with kidney links, short hame-tugs, straight panel pads, breastplates, trace bearers or loin straps optional, brown reins, bright steel pole chains. The hardware of the harness should be of the same metal as the polished metal parts of the vehicle. A standing martingale is required for a George IV Phaeton unless prohibited by individual class rules.

Attire: The driver usually wears a top hat, grey in summer, black in winter and in the evening indoors. A groom in livery occupies the rumble seat, but two grooms are considered proper with a Mail Phaeton. A Mail Phaeton may be turned out in country style with the wheel harness of a Road Coach and grooms in stable livery with derby hats. The driver would then wear clothes of country style.

Horses: The horses used with these phaetons are upstanding horses of appropriate size for the vehicle, with high, stylish action, yet showing a good length of stride. They should be horses of quality with adequate substance. It is not usual to have the manes braided.

5. FOUR-WHEELED DOG CART, TRAP, OUTING WAGON

Definition: These are informal vehicles of general utility. As such they may be painted to suit individual taste within the bounds of tradition and general practicality.

Harness: The harness may have a bridle with D-shaped winkers, with or without side-check bearing rein; Liverpool or elbow bit; Kay or rim collar and hames; hames may have connecting chain at bottom of hame straps both top and bottom, saddle of English pattern with French or Tilbury tugs for four-spring carriages, or as a saddle similar to Surrey harness for three- or end-spring carriages; breeching. Pair harness is similar, used with either trace bearers or breechings. Leather pole-straps are usual.

Attire: The driver wears country-style clothes with a derby, felt or straw hat according to season and weather. The groom wears stable livery with a derby hat. Horses: The horse, or horses, usually stands 15.2 to 15.3 hands, has good all-round straight action, good head carriage and possesses adequate substance for the weight of the vehicle. Good manners are important and the horse should be capable of trotting at a smart pace.

6. STANHOPE OR PARK GATE GIG

Definition: In North America these gigs were mostly used for show or park driving and were usually turned out in formal style.

Paint and bodywork: They are painted to a high finish with black body, patent leather dash and fenders, with the dummy louvers on the Park Gate type or the seat back painted in color. The undercarriage is painted in some quiet color, tastefully striped. These gigs are never finished in natural wood.

Harness: The harness has a bridle with square winkers, a gig or Buxton bit, sidecheck bearing rein, bridle fronts and rosettes of metal, Kay collar and well-fitted hames connected at the bottom with a chain and a ring. A breastplate or standing martingale is usual; the backstrap lined and stitched with the crupper sewn on; the saddle of English pattern with French or Tilbury tugs; a kicking strap is usually worn; brown driving reins. If the gig has a whiffletree, a breast collar of adequate size may be used.

Spares and appointments: Small lamps of square pattern are usual and a small kit of tools and a wheel wrench should be carried. A dashboard clock and a whip socket are desirable.

Horses: A gig horse should be an attractive horse standing 15.1 to 15.2 hands, of good conformation and bold head carriage. He should be sharp moving with high stylish action with a good length of stride that allows him to cover the ground at a good pace.

Attire: The driver wears a gray top hat in summer during daylight and a black top hat at other times. He wears an apron or knee rug. The groom wears dress livery.

7. VILLAGE CART, TWO-WHEELED DOG CART

Definition: These carts are usually made to seat four people, back to back. There is an adjustable seat to achieve the proper balance and the driver should have an adjustable foot-rest. The balance should be adjusted to bring a small amount of weight on the horse's back when the cart is loaded but not moving. The balance should NEVER be to the rear so that only the belly band prevents the cart from tipping up.

Paint and bodywork: The body is usually painted black and the shafts, springs and wheels in color and neatly striped.

Harness: The harness has a bridle with D-shaped winkers, a noseband and a Liverpool or similar bit. A four-ringed or Wilson snaffle may also be used, but a Buxton bit is too dressy for such carts. The collar may be of Kay or rim design with hames connected at the bottom by a chain for preference. A false martingale or breastplate is usual. The saddle should be made on a tree with an inside channel through which the backband can slide freely. Open tugs are usual. The saddle should be well padded and 4-1/2 or 5 inches wide. The back-strap may have the crupper buckled or sewn on. A breeching or kicking strap is usual.

Horses: The horse should be well muscled, have good clean bone and be of the right size for the cart. He should have good manners with free striding, straight action.

Attire: The driver and passengers may dress informally and the groom, if one is carried, wearing stable livery.

8. ROAD OR JOGGING CART

Definition: Light road carts are used for exercise and formerly they were sometimes used as personal conveyances like plain buggies. They may be painted to suit the individual's taste.

Harness: The harness is similar to buggy harness and usually has a bridle with an overdraw check and a snaffle bit. A bridle with a normal noseband and a double-ring or Wilson snaffle or a Liverpool bit is acceptable and may be preferred by some judges. Although the saddle has little weight to carry, it should be well enough stuffed so that no weight bears directly on the horse's spine. Horses: The usual road cart horse is of a fast trotting type.

9. FOUR-WHEELED BUGGY

Definition: This is a vehicle of general utility.

Paint and bodywork: The general style of painting was the body black and the running gear in some dark color with or without striping.

Harness: The harness should be of a simple kind with a bridle with square winkers, snaffle bit and overdraw check. A bridle with a noseband and a Wilson snaffle or a Liverpool bit is also quite appropriate. A breeching may or may not be used. Except for the heavier Goddard buggy, breast collars are usual.

Horses: The horse may be of trotting type, capable of moving at a good working trot. A pair may be driven to a buggy.

10. RUNABOUT, AMERICAN STANHOPE

Definition: These small vehicles were popular at the turn of the century and may be considered as light phaetons.

Paint and bodywork: Some were finished in natural wood, others were painted with a black body and undercarriage in sporting colors.

Harness: The harness has a bridle with D-shaped winkers, noseband and a Liverpool or elbow bit, preferably no bearing rein. A breast collar is usual and a breastplate is optional. A breeching is also optional. The harness should be of good quality with most straps lined and stitched. Brown reins.

Horses: The horse should be a stylishly moving horse of great quality, able to trot at a smart pace. High action is not essential.

11. ROCKAWAY, CARRYALL, DEPOT WAGON, SURREY, CABRIOLET

Definition: These are some of the types of family vehicles that were very popular throughout North America.

Paint and bodywork: They were usually painted in sober style with the body black, the undercarriage in some fairly dark color, tastefully striped. The cushions are usually covered in broadcloth of a color matching the undercarriage, or in black leather. The dash and fenders, if any, are usually covered with patent leather. A Surrey may have a standing top with a fringe. Most are fitted with shafts or a drop pole that attaches to couplings on the front axle.

Harness: The harness has a bridle with D-shaped winkers, bridle front of metal; side-check bearing rein or none at all; Liverpool or similar bit; collar of rim pattern with hames with chain connection at the bottom or with hamestraps at top and bottom; anchor or finger drafts; traces with slotted ends connected directly to the hames or to short hame tugs; saddle with straight or swell panels about 4 or 4-1/4 inches wide. Open or Tilbury tugs may be used and a breeching is normal. The harness straps may be lined and stitched or of single leather, the former preferred. A false martingale or breastplate is not essential. Pair harness is similar in style with short hame tugs and trace loops on the pads. Trace bearers are usual. A neck-yoke is used with a drop-pole, but if the pole is supported by a chain or strong spring, a crab pole-head and leather pole pieces may be used.

Horses: The horse (or horses) for a family vehicle should be 15.2 to 16 hands, with ample bone and weight for the work. High action is not wanted but a straight moving trot with a good length of stride and a regular active walk are what is needed. Good manners are essential.

12. COMMERCIAL VEHICLES

Definition: There is a wide variety of commercial vehicles used in the business of various trades. Each trade will have particular types and styles of vehicles, harness and horses suitable for that type of business.

Paint and bodywork: Vehicles are usually painted with signage indicating the proprietor, his location and the type of business and perhaps a business slogan.

Harness: The harness is well suited for the type of work and may also be decorated by the harness maker in order to attract attention and to be particularly memorable to the customers.

Horses: The horse (or horses) for a commercial vehicle should be especially suited for the type of business. Commercial turnouts should be asked only for walk, slow and working trot and are expected to be able to back and stand quietly. Good manners are essential.

(cited from: https://americandrivingsociety.org/Portals/ADS/2-8-20%20Redline%20book.pdf)

GLORIA'S TURNOUTS

DRIVING A TEAM OF FRIESIANS

I'm seen here in Lexington, Kentucky driving a four-in-hand of Friesian horses to a Healey Park Drag. Dr. Serra is by my side and Coachwoman, Melissa Warner, is riding on the front Gammon seat. The Grooms are Julie Riden and Nanette Elliott. I believe driving a large coach to four horses was and is the ultimate in carriage driving.

A CROSS TEAM (OR CHECKER BOARD)

Here I'm driving a cross team of Friesians and Kladruber horses, accompanied by Coachwoman Melissa Warner and grooms, Kacy Tipton and Susie Cramlet. We are at Blowing Rock, North Carolina. This turnout was sometimes called a "checkerboard." This was considered a valued alternative to the most prestigious of turnouts of all matching color.

DRIVING A "REVERSE" PIC AXE

WALNUT HILL FARM DRIVING COMPETITION

I serve with the CAA and as a CMA Board member and I can often be seen at their functions demonstrating unusual turnouts like this "Reverse" Pic Axe. Coachman, David Saunders and Groom, Michelle Dlugoborski are seen with me at John's Island in South Carolina.

Bringing home the first place blue ribbon was not uncommon when accompanied by Coachwoman, Melissa Warner and Groom, Kacy Tipton. I am seen here driving the leaders of my four-in-hand put to a roof seat break fitted for a pair. In these contests of four classes and a road drive, one has to accumulate more points than fellow competitor in the same division to win a championship.

ROAD COACH WITH COCK HORSE

DEMI-DAUMONT

At one of the Austin Horse Park Carriage and Horse Festivals, I presented four Kladrubers to a Lawton Road Coach. I am trailed by a Cock Horse which traditionally would have been positioned at the bottom of a hill to provide an extra horse power for the assent. The horse would have been hitched in front of the four and attached to the coach with a rope feeding between the two pairs of horses. Unhitched, the Cock Horse was returned to the bottom of the hill to wait for the next horse.

Coachwoman, Melissa Warner is riding the ride-horse in this Demi-Daumont turnout put to a Caleche by Muhlbacher of Paris. This presentation was part of a Carriage Association of America's Learning Weekend at the Austin Horse Park in Central Florida. Dr. Gene Serra is my escort. Kaylen Keathley is the groom on back seat.

A PIC AXE PUT TO CHAR-A-BANC

GIG TURNOUT

I'm driving a Char-a-banc by German manufacturer D.M. Mayer and I'm accompanied by Dr. Gene Serra. Driving five horses was in Eastern Europe was popular. The carriage size, load, or terrain often demanded extra horse power beyond four horses. The grooms here are Lynn Wingate and Nanette Elliott.

My granddaughter, Ms. Amy Lee, is here driving a Spanish Horse, stable name, Johnny, to the Park Gate Gig. She is accompanied by Coachman David Saunders. Most carriage horses are trained to travel pulling a carriage for one horse.

GRAND DAUMONT

CHANTILLY, FRANCE 2002

Coachwoman, Melissa Warner (riding the wheel ride-horse) and Senior Equine Specialist, Kacy Tipton (riding the lead ride-horse) are here featured as postilion riders with Nanette Elliott walking and Julie Riden riding in the dickie seat acting as footman. Originally footmen walked with a cane in front of a turnout to clear the way. This is called a Grand Daumont turnout put to a Caleche with a comfrey boot where the driver's seat would normally be positioned. The Caleche is manufactured by Muhlbacher of Paris.

I have been fortunate to drive in Traditional Driving shows at Chantilly's "Living Museum of the Horse" on three occasions. Here I am seen in 2002 driving a pair to an American Bronson Wagon with a platform or canape top restored by Patrick Schroven of Belgium. The Museum is located in the Great Stables built in 1719.

FOUR-IN-HAND

I'm driving a four-in-hand of Spanish horses to a Sport Break, accompanied by Dr. Gene Serra, and Coachman, David Saunders. The setting is Katrina Becker's farm in Windsor, South Carolina. The term "four-in-hand" means the four reins are held in one hand (the left) leaving the right hand free to manipulate the reins, direct the horses, or signal in traffic.

PIC AXE OR MEDIA POTENCIA

Fun with five in this configuration requires just four reins in one's hand. The two leader reins each have two coupling reins to cross to the leader on the right and left of the two outside horses. Driving four or five horses allows me to take a number of passengers and entertain guests in a unique fashion with a touch of elegance.

TWO-WHEELED COCKING CART "REVERSE" PIC AXE

DRIVING A CONCORD COACH

I'm driving five Friesians horses, accompanied by British Coachman, John Parker and groom, Michelle Dlugoborski. The rare two-wheeled cocking cart was owned by G. R.(Ray) Cormack, DVM and was reproduced from drawings from C. P. Kimble & Co. of Chicago, Illinois. This cart requires a unique configuration of three horses in the wheel position and two in the lead.

In this picture I'm driving a reproduction Concord Coach to four dark horses. This Eastern style coach is painted in the Wells Fargo colors, these coaches were used in the American West. Melissa Warner is riding in "shot gun" position and Lindsay Clark is grabbing a short ride on the step.

GLORIA'S DIAMOND

A LONG TEAM

Here I'm driving a turnout designed in early 2014 by myself and Coachman David Saunders. This turnout has never been presented before in history and is named after me. It is called "Gloria's Diamond."
This configuration was developed for a challenge by Friend, Gerard Paagman to do something unusual with horses.

Here I'm driving five horses called a Long Team. This configuration requires six reins held in the left hand with the right hand free to manipulate the reins and whip and operate the brake lever.
The horses have to be light on the bit (not pulling) and ready to pick up direction with the slightest of finger movement. My reins are sometimes called lady's reins since they are narrower to fit the smaller hand of a woman, although many men use this width rein.

SOURCES

Uses of vehicles today
https://www.carthrottle.com/post/7-reasons-why-americans-love-the-pickup-truck/
https://viralrang.com/why-people-like-sports-cars/
https://www.liveabout.com/reasons-why-people-buy-sport-utility-vehicles-3272218
http://frugalistablog.com/10-reasons-why-minivans-are-cool/
https://www.motortrend.com/news/five-reasons-get-sedan-crossover-five-reasons-not/

Definition
https://americandrivingsociety.org/Portals/ADS/Clean%20Book%20Web%202-11-20.pdf

Classification
https://fiveminutehistory.com/royal-carriages-traveling-in-splendor/
https://medium.com/@zacknorman97/shot-chaser-maserati-alfieri-shooting-brake-concept-d5992acf758a
https://web.archive.org/web/20071027142250/http://www.caaonline.com/caa_content.asp?PageType=Dept&Key=15&MCat=7
https://www.hotrod.com/articles/what-its-like-to-drive-a-tiller-truck/
https://fiveminutehistory.com/royal-carriages-traveling-in-splendor/ pix gala
https://nwcarriagemuseum.org/our-collection/
https://en.wikipedia.org/wiki/Postilion

Carriages
https://en.wikipedia.org/wiki/Carriage
https://en.wikipedia.org/wiki/Horse-drawn_vehicle
https://www.carriageassociationofamerica.com/the-quirky-history-of-the-meadowbrook/
https://americanhistory.si.edu/collections/search/object/nmah_325758
https://carriages-schroven.com/gallery/ pix
Bradney, J. (2005). The carriage-drive in Humphry Repton's landscapes. Garden History, 31-46.
https://www.slideshare.net/jeffthebat/carriages-by-catagory Gloria's carriage collection
http://www.britishdrivingsociety.co.uk/the-ralli-car/
https://www.thecarriagefoundation.org.uk/item/whitechapel-cart lots of px
https://aaqeastend.com/contents/portfolio/long-island-museum-carriage-collection-finest-collection-of-horse-drawn-vehicles/ lots of pix
https://www.kristenkoster.com/a-regency-era-carriage-primer/

https://shannondonnelly.com/2012/02/20/private-carraiges-of-the-english-regency/
https://www.carriageassociationofamerica.com/carriage-tour/roof-seat-break-or-char-a-banc/

Appointments
http://users.vermontel.net/~greenall/documents/APPOINTMENTSFORDRIVINGANTIQUECARRIAGES.pdf
https://www.farmauctionguide.com/alberta-auctions/estate-of-ted-swendson-carriage-auction-s-560887.html
lots of pix

People
http://www.aiat-driving.net/en/traditional-driving/the-turnout.html
https://horse-canada.com/horses-and-history/the-famous-british-mail-coaches-launched-by-the-theatre/
https://www.postalmuseum.org/blog/sound-of-the-post-horn/

Harness
https://ozarkcanada.wordpress.com/2011/03/24/fitting-the-harness-bridle/

www.ingramcontent.com/pod-product-compliance
Ingram Content Group UK Ltd.
Pitfield, Milton Keynes, MK11 3LW, UK
UKHW061139180426
11947UKWH00002B/6